Eucharistic
Prayers
for Concelebration

Eucharistic Prayers for Concelebration

Includes all Nine Eucharistic Prayers
Approved for Use
in the Dioceses of the United States of America
by the National Conference of Catholic Bishops
and Confirmed by the Apostolic See

ENGLISH TRANSLATION PREPARED BY THE
INTERNATIONAL COMMISSION ON ENGLISH IN THE LITURGY

CATHOLIC BOOK PUBLISHING CO.
New York

Concordat cum Originali:

Reverend John A. Gurrieri, Executive Director
Bishops' Committee on the Liturgy, National Conference of Catholic Bishops

Approved by the National Conference of Catholic Bishops for use in the dioceses of the United States of America, November 13, 1973. Confirmed by decree of the Congregation for Divine Worship, February 4, 1973 (Prot. N. CD 1762/73).

Revised according to the second typical edition of the *Missale Romanum* (1975), March 1, 1985, for use in the dioceses of the United States of America.

Published by Authority of the Bishop's Committee on the Liturgy, National Conference of Catholic Bishops.

The English translation of Eucharistic Prayers, I, II, III, and IV and the Confiteor from the *Roman Missal* copyright © 1973, International Committee on English in the Liturgy, Inc.; the English translation of the *Eucharistic Prayers for Masses with Children* © 1975, ICEL; the English translation of the *Eucharistic Prayers for Masses of Reconciliation* © 1975, ICEL; excerpts from the English translation of the General Instruction of the Roman Missal from *Documents on the Liturgy, 1963-1979: Conciliar, Papal, and Curial Texts* © 1982, ICEL.

The English translations of the Gloria, the Apostles' Creed, and the Nicene Creed by the International Consultation on English Texts.

(T-24)

INTRODUCTION

One of the fruits of the liturgical reform of the Second Vatican Council was the restoration of concelebration as a regular part of the life of the Latin Church.

Concelebration effectively brings out the unity of the priesthood, of the sacrifice, and of the whole people of God [153]*.

The structure of a concelebrated Mass, whatever its form, follows the norms for an individual celebration, except for the points prescribed or changed by the General Instruction of the Roman Missal [159].

One of the parts of the Mass that is specifically modified by concelebration is the eucharistic prayer.

EUCHARISTIC PRAYER

Now the center and summit of the entire celebration begins: the eucharistic prayer, a prayer of thanksgiving and sanctification. The priest invites the people to lift up their hearts to the Lord in prayer and thanks; he unites them with himself in the prayer he addresses in their name to the Father through Jesus Christ. The meaning of the prayer is that the entire congregation joins itself to Christ in acknowledging the great things God has done and in offering the sacrifice [54].

The chief elements making up the eucharistic prayer are these:

a) *Thanksgiving* (expressed especially in the preface): in the name of the entire people of God, the priest praises the Father and gives thanks to him for the whole work of salvation or for some special aspect of it that corresponds to the day, feast, or season.

b) *Acclamation:* joining with the angels, the congregation sings or recites the *Sanctus.* This acclamation is an intrinsic part of the eucharistic prayer and all the people join with the priest in singing or reciting it.

c) *Epiclesis:* in special invocations the Church calls on God's power and asks that the gifts offered by human hands be consecrated, that is, become Christ's body and blood, and that the victim to be received in communion be the source of salvation for those who will partake.

d) *Institution narrative and consecration:* in the words and actions of Christ, that sacrifice is celebrated which he himself instituted at the Last Supper, when, under the appearances of bread and wine, he offered his body and blood, gave them to his apostles to eat and drink, then he commanded that they carry on this mystery.

---

* Unless otherwise indicated, the numbers in the brackets refer to the *General Instruction of the Roman Missal.*

e) *Anamnesis:* in fulfillment of the command received from Christ through the apostles, the Church keeps his memorial by recalling especially his passion, resurrection, and ascension.

f) *Offering:* in this memorial, the Church—and in particular the Church here and now assembled—offers the spotless victim to the Father in the Holy Spirit. The Church's intention is that the faithful not only offer this victim but also learn to offer themselves and so to surrender themselves, through Christ the Mediator, to an ever more complete union with the Father and with each other, so that at last God may be all in all.

g) *Intercessions:* the intercessions make it clear that the eucharist is celebrated in communion with the entire Church and all its members, living and dead, who are called to share in the salvation and redemption purchased by Christ's body and blood.

h) *Final doxology:* the praise of God is expressed in the doxology, to which the people's acclamation is an assent and a conclusion.

The eucharistic prayer calls for all to listen in silent reverence, but also to take part through the acclamations for which the rite makes provision [55].

MANNER OF RECITING THE EUCHARISTIC PRAYER

The priest then begins the eucharistic prayer. With hands outstretched, he says: *The Lord be with you.* As he says: *Lift up your hearts,* he raises his hands; with hands outstretched, he adds: *Let us give thanks to the Lord our God.* When the people have answered, *It is right to give him thanks and praise,* the priest continues the preface. At its conclusion, he joins his hands and sings or says aloud with the ministers and people the *Sanctus-Benedictus* (see no. 55) [108].

The priest continues the eucharistic prayer according to the rubrics that are given for each of them. If the priest celebrant is a bishop, after the words *N. our Pope* or the equivalent, he adds: *and for me your unworthy servant.* The local Ordinary must be mentioned in this way: *N. our Bishop* (or Vicar, Prelate, Prefect, Abbot). Coadjutor and auxiliary bishops may be mentioned in the eucharistic prayer. When several are named, this is done with the collective formula, *N. our bishop and his assistant bishops.* All these phrases should be modified grammatically to fit each of the eucharistic prayers.

A little before the consecration, the server may ring a bell as a signal to the faithful. Depending on local custom, he also rings the bell at the showing of the host and the chalice [109].

MANNER OF RECITING THE EUCHARISTIC PRAYER
AT CONCELEBRATED MASSES

The preface is said by the principal celebrant alone; the *Sanctus* is sung or recited by all the concelebrants with the congregation and choir [168].

After the *Sanctus,* the concelebrants continue the eucharistic prayer in the way to be described. Unless otherwise indicated, only the principal celebrant makes the gestures [169].

The parts said by the concelebrants together are to be recited in such a way that the concelebrants say them in a softer voice and the principal celebrant's voice stands out clearly. In this way the congregation should be able to hear the text without difficulty [170].

A. Eucharistic Prayer I, The Roman Canon

The prayer, *We come to you, Father,* is said by the principal celebrant alone, with hands outstretched [171].

The intercessions, *Remember, Lord, your people* and *In union with the whole Church,* may be assigned to one of the concelebrants; he alone says these prayers, with hands outstretched and aloud [172].

The prayer, *Father, accept this offering,* is said by the principal celebrant alone, with hands outstretched [173].

From *Bless and approve our offering,* to *Almighty God, we pray* inclusive, all the concelebrants recite everything together in this manner:

a) They say *Bless and approve our offering* with hands outstretched toward the offerings.

b) They say *The day before he suffered* and *When supper was ended* with hands joined.

c) While saying the words of the Lord, each extends his right hand toward the bread and toward the chalice, if this seems appropriate; they look at the eucharistic bread and chalice as these are shown and afterward bow low.

d) They say *Father, we celebrate the memory of Christ* and *Look with favor* with hands outstretched.

e) From *Almighty God, we pray* to *the sacred body and blood of your Son* inclusive, they bow with hands joined; then they stand upright and cross themselves at the words, *let us be filled* [174].

The intercessions, *Remember, Lord, those who have died* and *For ourselves, too,* may be assigned to one of the concelebrants; he alone says these prayers, with hands outstretched and aloud [175].

At the words, *Though we are sinners,* all the concelebrants strike their breast [176].

The prayer, *Through Christ our Lord you give us all these gifts,* is said by the principal celebrant alone [177].

In this eucharistic prayer the parts from *Bless and approve our offering* to *Almighty God, we pray* inclusive and the concluding doxology may be sung [178].

B. Eucharistic Prayer II

The prayer, *Lord, you are holy indeed,* is said by the principal celebrant alone, with hands outstretched [179].

From *Let your Spirit come* to *May all of us who share* inclusive, all the concelebrants together say the prayer in this manner:

a) They say *Let your Spirit come* with hands outstretched toward the offerings.

b) They say *Before he was given up to death* and *When supper was ended* with hands joined.

c) While saying the words of the Lord, each extends his right hand toward the bread and toward the chalice, if this seems appropriate; they look at the eucharistic bread and the chalice as they are shown and afterward bow low.

d) They say *In memory of his death* and *May all of us who share* with hands outstretched [180].

The intercessions for the living, *Lord, remember your Church,* and for the dead, *Remember our brothers and sisters,* may be assigned to one of the concelebrants; he alone says the intercessions, with hands outstretched [181].

In this eucharistic prayer the parts from *Before he was given up to death* to *In memory of his death* inclusive and the concluding doxology may be sung [182].

C. Eucharistic Prayer III

The prayer, *Father, you are holy indeed* is said by the principal celebrant alone, with hands outstretched [183].

From *And so, Father, we bring you these gifts* to *Look with favor* inclusive, all the concelebants together say the prayer in this manner:

a) They say *And so, Father, we bring you these gifts* with hands outstretched toward the offerings.

b) They say *On the night he was betrayed* and *When supper was ended* with hands joined.

c) While saying the words of the Lord, each extends his right hand toward the bread and toward the chalice, if this seems appropriate; they look at the eucharistic bread and chalice as these are shown and afterward bow low.

d) They say *Father, calling to mind* and *Look with favor* with hands outstretched [184].

The intercessions, *May he make us an everlasting gift* and *Lord may this sacrifice,* may be assigned to one of the concelebrants; he alone says these prayers, with hands outstretched [185].

In this eucharistic prayer the parts from *On the night he was betrayed* to *Father, calling to mind* inclusive and the concluding doxology may be sung [186].

D. Eucharistic Prayer IV

The prayer, *Father, we acknowledge,* is said by the principal celebrant alone, with hands outstretched [187].

From *Father, may this Holy Spirit* to *Lord, look upon this sacrifice* inclusive, all the concelebrants together say the prayer in this manner:

a) They say *Father, may this Holy Spirit* with hands outstretched toward the offerings.

b) They say *He always loved those* and *In the same way* with hands joined.

c) While saying the words of the Lord, each extends his right hand toward the bread and toward the chalice, if this seems appropriate; they look at the eucharistic bread and chalice as these are shown and afterward bow low.

d) They say *Father, we now celebrate* and *Lord, look upon this sacrifice* with hands outstretched [188].

The intercessions, *Lord, remember those,* may be assigned to one of the concelebrants; he alone says them, with hands outstretched [189].

In this eucharistic prayer the parts from *He always loved those* to *Father, we now celebrate* inclusive and the concluding doxology may be sung [190].

The concluding doxology of the eucharistic prayer may be sung or said either by the principal celebrant alone or together with all the concelebrants [191].

Eucharistic Prayers for Masses with Children

Although the eucharistic prayers for Masses with children are contained in this booklet, in view of the psychology of children it seems better to refrain from concelebration when Mass is celebrated with children [22, Eucharistic Prayers for Masses with Children].

If there is sufficient reason to have a concelebrated Mass with children the rubrics contained in each prayer are followed.

Eucharistic Prayers for Masses of Reconciliation

For concelebration, these eucharistic prayers are said in the following way:

A. Eucharistic Prayer I

a) The preface is said by the celebrant alone, with hands extended.

b) From *Look with kindness on your people* to *healed of all division,* all the concelebrants say the prayer together.

From *send forth the power of your Spirit* to *in whom we have become your sons and daughters,* the concelebrants extend their right hands toward the offerings. While saying the words of the Lord, each extends his right hand toward the bread and toward the chalice, if this seems opportune.

c) The intercession *Keep us all* to *with Christ, our risen Lord* may be assigned to one of the concelebrants; he alone says the intercession with hands extended.

B. Eucharistic Prayer II

a) The preface is said by the celebrant alone, with hands extended.

God of power and might to *and find our way to one another* is also said by the celebrant alone, with hands extended.

b) From *Therefore we celebrate the reconciliation* to *take away all that divides us,* all the concelebrants say the prayer together.

From *We ask you to sanctify* to *your Son's ✙ command,* the concelebrants extend their hands toward the offerings. While saying the words of the Lord, each extends his right hand toward the bread and toward the chalice if this seems opportune.

c) The intercessions *May this Spirit* and *You have gathered us here* may be assigned to one or other of the concelebrants who alone says the intercessions with hands extended.

CONTENTS

EUCHARISTIC
PRAYERS
I
II
III
IV

EUCHARISTIC PRAYER I

(ROMAN CANON)

In this eucharistic prayer, the words in brackets may be omitted.

The principal celebrant, with hands extended, says:

**We come to you, Father,
with praise and thanksgiving,
through Jesus Christ your Son.
Through him we ask you to accept and bless ✚
these gifts we offer you in sacrifice.
We offer them for your holy catholic Church,
watch over it, Lord, and guide it;
grant it peace and unity throughout the world.
We offer them for N. our Pope,
for N. our bishop, ***
**and for all who hold and teach the catholic faith
that comes to us from the apostles.**

Celebrant alone

COMMEMORATION OF THE LIVING

With hands extended, he says:

*Celebrant or
one concelebrant*

**Remember, Lord, your people,
especially those for whom we now pray, N. and N.**

With hands joined, he prays for them briefly.

Then, with hands extended, he continues:

SPECIAL FORM of In Union with the whole Church (Communicantes)

CHRISTMAS AND DURING THE OCTAVE

In union with the whole Church
we celebrate that day (night)
when Mary without loss of her virginity
gave the world its savior.
We honor Mary,
the ever-virgin mother of Jesus Christ our Lord and God.†

HOLY THURSDAY

In union with the whole Church
we celebrate that day
when Jesus Christ, our Lord,
was betrayed for us.
We honor Mary,
the ever-virgin mother of Jesus Christ our Lord and God.†

EPIPHANY

In union with the whole Church
we celebrate that day
when your only Son,
sharing your eternal glory,
showed himself in a human body.
We honor Mary,
the ever-virgin mother of Jesus Christ our
   Lord and God.†

* When several are to be named, a general form is used: for N. our bishop and his assistant bishops, as in number 172 of the General Instruction.

14

Remember all of us gathered here before you.
You know how firmly we believe in you
and dedicate ourselves to you.
We offer you this sacrifice of praise
for ourselves and those who are dear to us.
We pray to you, our living and true God,
for our well-being and redemption.

He joins his hands.

With hands extended, he says:

In union with the whole Church
we honor Mary,
the ever-virgin mother of Jesus Christ our Lord and God.
† We honor Joseph, her husband,
the apostles and martyrs
Peter and Paul, Andrew,
[James, John, Thomas,
James, Philip,
Bartholomew, Matthew, Simon and Jude;
we honor Linus, Cletus, Clement, Sixtus,
Cornelius, Cyprian, Lawrence, Chrysogonus,
John and Paul, Cosmas and Damian]
and all the saints.
May their merits and prayers
gain us your constant help and protection.
[Through Christ our Lord. Amen.]

Celebrant or one concelebrant

**FROM THE EASTER VIGIL TO THE
SECOND SUNDAY OF EASTER INCLUSIVE**

In union with the whole Church
we celebrate that day (night)
when Jesus Christ, our Lord,
rose from the dead in his human body.
We honor Mary,
the ever-virgin mother of Jesus Christ our
    Lord and God.†

PENTECOST

In union with the whole Church
we celebrate the day of Pentecost
when the Holy Spirit appeared to the apostles
in the form of countless tongues.
We honor Mary,
the ever-virgin mother of Jesus Christ our
    Lord and God.†

ASCENSION

In union with the whole Church
we celebrate that day
when your Son, our Lord,
took his place with you

and raised our frail human nature to glory.
We honor Mary,
the ever-virgin mother of Jesus Christ our
    Lord and God.†

With hands extended, the principal celebrant continues:

Father, accept this offering   Celebrant alone
from your whole family.
Grant us your peace in this life,
save us from final damnation,
and count us among those you have chosen.

He joins his hands.

[Through Christ our Lord. Amen.]

All concelebrants, with hands outstretched over the offerings, say:

Bless and approve our offering;   Celebrant
make it acceptable to you,   with concelebrants
an offering in spirit and in truth.
Let it become for us
the body and blood of Jesus Christ,
your only Son, our Lord.

They join their hands.

[Through Christ our Lord. Amen.]

The day before he suffered *
he took bread in his sacred hands
and looking up to heaven,
to you, his almighty Father,
he gave you thanks and praise.
He broke the bread,
gave it to his disciples, and said:

SPECIAL FORM of Father, accept this offering (Hanc igitur)

HOLY THURSDAY
Father, accept this offering
from your whole family
in memory of the day when Jesus Christ, our Lord,
gave the mysteries of his body and blood
for his disciples to celebrate. Grant us . . .

FROM THE EASTER VIGIL TO THE SECOND
SUNDAY OF EASTER INCLUSIVE
Father, accept this offering
from your whole family
and from those born into the new life
of water and the Holy Spirit,
with all their sins forgiven. Grant us . . .

* HOLY THURSDAY
The day before he suffered
to save us and all men,
that is today,

Each extends his right hand towards the bread, if this seems opportune.

Take this, all of you, and eat it:
this is my body which will be given up for you.

At the elevation they look at the host and afterwards bow low.

Then all continue:

When supper was ended,
he took the cup.
Again he gave you thanks and praise,
gave the cup to his disciples, and said:

Each extends his right hand towards the chalice, if this seems opportune.

Take this, all of you, and drink from it:
this is the cup of my blood,
the blood of the new and everlasting covenant.
It will be shed for you and for all
so that sins may be forgiven.
Do this in memory of me.

At the elevation they look at the chalice and afterwards bow low.

Then the principal celebrant sings or says:

Celebrant alone

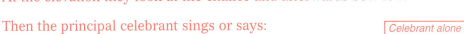

Let us pro-claim the mys-te-ry of faith:

People with celebrant
or concelebrants

A

Christ has died, Christ is ris - en, Christ will come a - gain.

B Dying you destroyed our death,
rising you restored our life.
Lord Jesus, come in glory.

C When we eat this bread and drink this cup,
we proclaim your death, Lord Jesus,
until you come in glory.

D Lord, by your cross and resurrection
you have set us free.
You are the Savior of the world.

With hands extended, all say:

Father, we celebrate the memory of Christ, your Son.
We, your people and your ministers,
recall his passion,
his resurrection from the dead,
and his ascension into glory;
and from the many gifts you have given us
we offer to you, God of glory and majesty,
this holy and perfect sacrifice:
the bread of life
and the cup of eternal salvation.

Look with favor on these offerings
and accept them as once you accepted
the gifts of your servant Abel,
the sacrifice of Abraham, our father in faith,
and the bread and wine offered by your priest Melchisedech.

Bowing, with hands joined, all continue:

Almighty God,
we pray that your angel may take this sacrifice
to your altar in heaven.
Then, as we receive from this altar
the sacred body and blood of your Son,

They stand up straight and make the sign of the cross, saying:

let us be filled with every grace and blessing.

They join their hands.

[Through Christ our Lord. Amen.]

COMMEMORATION OF THE DEAD

With hands extended, he says:

Remember, Lord, those who have died
and have gone before us marked with the sign of faith,
especially those for whom we now pray, **N.** and **N.**

With hands joined, he prays for them briefly.

Then, with hands extended, he continues:

> May these, and all who sleep in Christ,
> find in your presence
> light, happiness, and peace.

He joins his hands.

> [Through Christ our Lord. Amen.]

With hands extended, he says:

Celebrant or one concelebrant

> **F**or ourselves, too, we ask
> some share in the fellowship of your apostles and martyrs,
> with John the Baptist, Stephen, Matthias, Barnabas,
>> [Ignatius, Alexander, Marcellinus, Peter,
>> Felicity, Perpetua, Agatha, Lucy,
>> Agnes, Cecilia, Anastasia]
> and all the saints.

All strike their breast with the right hand:

> Though we are sinners,
> we trust in your mercy and love.

With hands extended as before, he continues:

> Do not consider what we truly deserve,
> but grant us your forgiveness.

He joins his hands.

> Through Christ our Lord.

He continues:

Celebrant alone

> **T**hrough him you give us all these gifts.
> You fill them with life and goodness,
> you bless them and make them holy.

Celebrant alone or with concelebrants

The principal celebrant takes the paten with the host and the deacon (or in his absence one of the concelebrants) takes the chalice and, lifting them up, the principal celebrant sings or says alone or with the concelebrants:

Through him, with him, in him, in the u - ni - ty of the Ho - ly Spir-it,

all glo-ry and hon-or is yours, al-might-y Fa - ther, for ev - er and ev - er.

The people respond: ℟. A - men.

EUCHARISTIC PRAYER II

Priest: **The Lord be with you.**
People: And also with you.

Priest: **Lift up your hearts.**
People: We lift them up to the Lord.

Priest: **Let us give thanks to the Lord our God.**
People: It is right to give him thanks and praise.

Father, it is our duty and our salvation, always and everywhere to give you thanks through your beloved Son, Jesus Christ.

Celebrant alone

He is the Word through whom you made the universe, the Savior you sent to redeem us. By the power of the Holy Spirit he took flesh and was born of the Virgin Mary.

For our sake he opened his arms on the cross; he put an end to death and revealed the resurrection. In this he fulfilled your will and won for you a holy people.

And so we join the angels and the saints in proclaiming your glory as we say:

People with celebrant and concelebrants

Holy, holy, holy Lord, God of power and might, heaven and earth are full of your glory.
    Hosanna in the highest.
Blessed is he who comes in the name of the Lord.
    Hosanna in the highest.

The principal celebrant, with hands extended, says:

Lord, you are holy indeed,
the fountain of all holiness.

He joins his hands.

All concelebrants, with hands outstretched over the offerings, say:

**Let your Spirit come upon these gifts to make them holy,
so that they may become for us
the body ✠ and blood of our Lord, Jesus Christ.**

They join their hands.

Before he was given up to death,
a death he freely accepted,
he took bread and gave you thanks.
He broke the bread,
gave it to his disciples, and said:

Each extends his right hand towards the bread, if this seems opportune.

**Take this, all of you, and eat it:
this is my body which will be given up for you.**

At the elevation they look at the host and afterwards bow low.

Then all continue:

When supper was ended, he took the cup.
Again he gave you thanks and praise,
gave the cup to his disciples, and said:

Each extends his right hand towards the chalice, if this seems opportune.

**Take this, all of you, and drink from it:
this is the cup of my blood,
the blood of the new and everlasting covenant.
It will be shed for you and for all
so that sins may be forgiven.
Do this in memory of me.**

At the elevation they look at the chalice and afterwards bow low.

Then the principal celebrant sings or says: *Celebrant alone*

Let us pro-claim the mys-te-ry of faith:

A   *People with celebrant or concelebrants*

Christ has died, Christ is ris - en, Christ will come   a - gain.

B Dying you destroyed our death,
rising you restored our life.
Lord Jesus, come in glory.

D Lord, by your cross and resurrection
you have set us free.
You are the Savior of the world.

C When we eat this bread and drink this cup,
we proclaim your death, Lord Jesus,
until you come in glory.

With hands extended, all say:

In memory of his death and resurrection,
we offer you, Father, this life-giving bread,   *Celebrant with concelebrants*
this saving cup.
We thank you for counting us worthy
to stand in your presence and serve you.
May all of us who share in the body and blood of Christ
be brought together in unity by the Holy Spirit.

With hands extended, he says: *Celebrant or one concelebrant*

Lord, remember your Church throughout the world;
make us grow in love,
together with **N.** our Pope,
N. our bishop,* and all the clergy.

In Masses for the dead the following may be added:
**Remember N., whom you have called from this life.
In baptism he (she) died with Christ:
may he (she) also share his resurrection.**

* When several are to be named, a general form is used for N. our bishop
and his assistant bishops, as in number 172 of the General Instruction.

With hands extended, he says:

Remember our brothers and sisters
who have gone to their rest
in the hope of rising again;
bring them and all the departed
into the light of your presence.
Have mercy on us all;
make us worthy to share eternal life
with Mary, the virgin Mother of God,
with the apostles, and with all the saints
who have done your will throughout the ages.
May we praise you in union with them,
and give you glory

Celebrant or one concelebrant

He joins his hands.

through your Son, Jesus Christ.

The principal celebrant takes the paten with the host and the deacon (or in his absence one of the concelebrants) takes the chalice and, lifting them up, the principal celebrant sings or says alone or with the concelebrants:

Celebrant alone or with concelebrants

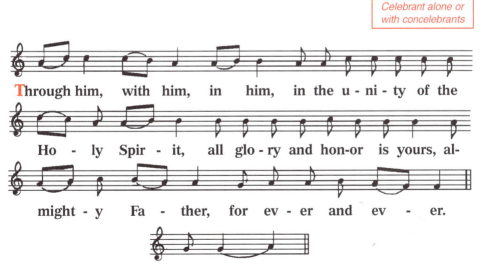

Through him, with him, in him, in the u-ni-ty of the Ho-ly Spir-it, all glo-ry and hon-or is yours, al-might-y Fa-ther, for ev-er and ev-er.

The people respond: ℟. A - men.

EUCHARISTIC PRAYER III

The principal celebrant, with hands extended, says:

Father, you are holy indeed,
 and all creation rightly gives you praise.
All life, all holiness comes from you
through your Son, Jesus Christ our Lord,
by the working of the Holy Spirit.
From age to age you gather a people to yourself,
so that from east to west
a perfect offering may be made
to the glory of your name.

Celebrant alone

He joins his hands.

All concelebrants, with hands outstretched over the offerings, say:

*Celebrant
with concelebrants*

And so, Father, we bring you these gifts.
 We ask you to make them holy by the power of your Spirit,
that they may become the body ✠ and blood
of your Son, our Lord Jesus Christ,
at whose command we celebrate this eucharist.

They join their hands.

On the night he was betrayed,
 he took bread and gave you thanks and praise.
He broke the bread, gave it to his disciples, and said:

Each extends his right hand towards the bread, if this seems opportune.

**Take this, all of you, and eat it:
this is my body which will be given up for you.**

At the elevation they look at the host and afterwards bow low.

Then all continue:

When supper was ended, he took the cup.
Again he gave you thanks and praise,
gave the cup to his disciples, and said:

Each extends his right hand towards the chalice, if this seems opportune.

**Take this, all of you, and drink from it:
this is the cup of my blood,
the blood of the new and everlasting covenant.
It will be shed for you and for all
so that sins may be forgiven.
Do this in memory of me.**

At the elevation they look at the chalice and afterwards bow low.

Then the principal celebrant sings or says:

Celebrant alone

Let us pro-claim the mys-te-ry of faith:

People with celebrant or concelebrants

A

Christ has died, Christ is ris - en, Christ will come a - gain.

B Dying you destroyed our death,
rising you restored our life.
Lord Jesus, come in glory.

C When we eat this bread and drink this cup,
we proclaim your death, Lord Jesus,
until you come in glory.

D Lord, by your cross and resurrection
you have set us free.
You are the Savior of the world.

With hands extended, all say:

Celebrant with concelebrants

Father, calling to mind the death your Son endured for
   our salvation,
his glorious resurrection and ascension into heaven,
and ready to greet him when he comes again,
we offer you in thanksgiving this holy and living sacrifice.

Look with favor on your Church's offering,
   and see the Victim whose death has reconciled us to
     yourself.
Grant that we, who are nourished by his body and blood,
may be filled with his Holy Spirit,
and become one body, one spirit in Christ.

With hands extended, he says:

Celebrant or one concelebrant

May he make us an everlasting gift to you
   and enable us to share in the inheritance of your saints,
with Mary, the virgin Mother of God;
with the apostles, the martyrs,
(Saint N.—the saint of the day or the patron saint)
     and all your saints,
on whose constant intercession we rely for help.

With hands extended, he says:

Celebrant or one concelebrant

Lord, may this sacrifice,
   which has made our peace with you,
advance the peace and salvation of all the world.
Strengthen in faith and love your pilgrim Church on earth;
your servant, Pope N., our bishop N., *
and all the bishops,
with the clergy and the entire people your Son has gained for
     you.
Father, hear the prayers of the family you have gathered here
     before you.
In mercy and love unite all your children wherever
     they may be. * *

 * When several are to be named, a general form is used: for N. our bishop
and his assistant bishops, as in number 172 of the General Instruction.

* * In Masses for the dead, see page 27.

Welcome into your kingdom our departed brothers and sisters, and all who have left this world in your friendship.

He joins his hands.

We hope to enjoy for ever the vision of your glory,
through Christ our Lord, from whom all good things come.

The principal celebrant takes the paten with the host and the deacon (or in his absence one of the concelebrants) takes the chalice and, lifting them up, the principal celebrant sings or says alone or with the concelebrants:

Celebrant alone or with concelebrants

Through him, with him, in him, in the u - ni - ty of the Ho - ly Spir-it,

all glo-ry and hon-or is yours, al-might-y   Fa - ther, for ev - er and ev - er.

The people respond:  R̶. A - men.

---

* * When this eucharistic prayer is used in Masses for the dead, the following may be said:

Remember **N.**
In baptism he **(she)** died with Christ:
may he **(she)** also share his resurrection,
when Christ will raise our mortal bodies
and make them like his own in glory.

Welcome into your kingdom our departed brothers and sisters,
and all who have left this world in your friendship.
There we hope to share in your glory
when every tear will be wiped away.
On that day we shall see you, our God, as you are.

He joins his hands.

We shall become like you
and praise you for ever through Christ our Lord,
from whom all good things come.

He takes the chalice and the paten with the host and, lifting them up, says:

Through him, etc. as above.

EUCHARISTIC PRAYER IV

Priest: **The Lord be with you.**
People: And also with you.

Priest: **Lift up your hearts.**
People: We lift them up to the Lord.

Priest: **Let us give thanks to the Lord our God.**
People: It is right to give him thanks and praise.

Celebrant alone

Father in heaven,
it is right that we should give you thanks and glory:
you are the one God, living and true.
Through all eternity you live in unapproachable light.
Source of life and goodness, you have created all things,
to fill your creatures with every blessing
and lead all men to the joyful vision of your light.
Countless hosts of angels stand before you to do your will;
they look upon your splendor
and praise you, night and day.
United with them,
and in the name of every creature under heaven,
we too praise your glory as we say:

*People with celebrant
and concelebrants*

Holy, holy, holy Lord, God of power and might,
heaven and earth are full of your glory.
  Hosanna in the highest.
Blessed is he who comes in the name of the Lord.
  Hosanna in the highest.

The principal celebrant, with hands extended, says:

Celebrant alone

Father, we acknowledge your greatness:
all your actions show your wisdom and love.
You formed man in your own likeness
and set him over the whole world
to serve you, his creator,
and to rule over all creatures.
Even when he disobeyed you and lost your friendship
you did not abandon him to the power of death,
but helped all men to seek and find you.
Again and again you offered a covenant to man,
and through the prophets taught him to hope for salvation.
Father, you so loved the world
that in the fullness of time you sent your only Son to be
our Savior.

He was conceived through the power of the Holy Spirit,
and born of the Virgin Mary,
a man like us in all things but sin.
To the poor he proclaimed the good news of salvation,
to prisoners, freedom,
and to those in sorrow, joy.
In fulfillment of your will
he gave himself up to death;
but by rising from the dead,
he destroyed death and restored life.
And that we might live no longer for ourselves but for him,
he sent the Holy Spirit from you, Father,
as his first gift to those who believe,
to complete his work on earth
and bring us the fullness of grace.

He joins his hands.

All concelebrants, with hands outstretched over the offerings, say:

Father, may this Holy Spirit sanctify these offerings.
Let them become the body ✠ and blood of Jesus
   Christ our Lord

They join their hands.

as we celebrate the great mystery
which he left us as an everlasting covenant.

He always loved those who were his own in the world.
When the time came for him to be glorified by you,
      his heavenly Father,
he showed the depth of his love.

While they were at supper,
he took bread, said the blessing, broke the bread,
and gave it to his disciples, saying:

Each extends his right hand towards the bread, if this seems opportune.

Take this, all of you, and eat it:
this is my body which will be given up for you.

At the elevation they look at the host and afterwards bow low.

Then all continue:

In the same way, he took the cup, filled with wine.
He gave you thanks, and giving the cup to his disciples,
      said:

Each extends his right hand towards the chalice, if this seems opportune.

Take this, all of you, and drink from it:
this is the cup of my blood,
the blood of the new and everlasting covenant.
It will be shed for you and for all
so that sins may be forgiven.
Do this in memory of me.

At the elevation they look at the chalice and afterwards bow low.

Then the principal celebrant sings or says:

Celebrant alone

Let us pro-claim the mys-te-ry of faith:

People with celebrant or concelebrants

A

Christ has died, Christ is ris - en, Christ will come a - gain.

B Dying you destroyed our death,
rising you restored our life.
Lord Jesus, come in glory.

D Lord, by your cross and resurrection
you have set us free.
You are the Savior of the world.

C When we eat this bread and drink this cup,
we proclaim your death, Lord Jesus,
until you come in glory.

With hands extended, all say:

Celebrant with concelebrants

Father, we now celebrate this memorial of our redemption.
We recall Christ's death, his descent among the dead,
his resurrection, and his ascension to your right hand;
and, looking forward to his coming in glory,
we offer you his body and blood,
the acceptable sacrifice
which brings salvation to the whole world.

Lord, look upon this sacrifice which you have given to
your Church;
and by your Holy Spirit, gather all who share this one bread
and one cup
into the one body of Christ, a living sacrifice of praise.

With hands extended, he says:

Lord, remember those for whom we offer this sacrifice,
especially N. our Pope,
N. our bishop, *and bishops and clergy everywhere.
Remember those who take part in this offering,
those here present and all your people,
and all who seek you with a sincere heart.
Remember those who have died in the peace of Christ
and all the dead whose faith is known to you alone.
Father, in your mercy grant also to us, your children,
to enter into our heavenly inheritance
in the company of the Virgin Mary, the Mother of God,
and your apostles and saints.
Then, in your kingdom, freed from the corruption of sin
        and death,
we shall sing your glory with every creature through
        Christ our Lord,

He joins his hands.

through whom you give us everything that is good.

The principal celebrant takes the paten with the host and the deacon (or in his absence one of the concelebrants) takes the chalice and, lifting them up, the principal celebrant sings or says alone or with the concelebrants:

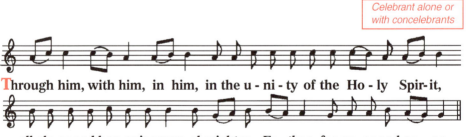

Through him, with him, in him, in the u - ni - ty of the Ho - ly   Spir-it,

all glo-ry and hon-or is yours, al-might-y   Fa - ther, for ev - er and ev - er.

The people respond: ℟. A - men.

* When several are to be named, a general form is used: for N. our bishop and his assistant bishops, as in number 172 of the General Instruction.

EUCHARISTIC PRAYERS
FOR MASSES WITH CHILDREN
C 1
C 2
C 3

●

EUCHARISTIC
PRAYERS
FOR MASSES OF RECONCILIATION
R 1
R 2

EUCHARISTIC PRAYER
FOR MASSES WITH CHILDREN

I

Priest: **The Lord be with you.**
People: And also with you.

Priest: **Lift up your hearts.**
People: We lift them up to the Lord.

Priest: **Let us give thanks to the Lord our God.**
People: It is right to give him thanks and praise.

The principal celebrant, with hands extended, says:

God our Father,
you have brought us here together
so that we can give you thanks and praise
for all the wonderful things you have done.

Celebrant alone

We thank you for all that is beautiful in the world
and for the happiness you have given us.
We praise you for daylight
and for your word which lights up our minds.
We praise you for the earth,
and all the people who live on it,
and for our life which comes from you.

We know that you are good.
You love us and do great things for us.
[So we all sing (say) together:

People with celebrant and concelebrants

Holy, holy, holy Lord, God of power and might,
heaven and earth are full of your glory.
Hosanna in the highest.]

34

With hands extended, he says:

Father,   *Celebrant alone*
you are always thinking about your people;
you never forget us.
You sent us your Son Jesus,
who gave his life for us
and who came to save us.
He cured sick people;
he cared for those who were poor
and wept with those who were sad.
He forgave sinners
and taught us to forgive each other.
He loved everyone
and showed us how to be kind.
He took children in his arms and blessed them.
[So we are glad to sing (say):

*People with celebrant
and concelebrants*

Blessed is he who comes in the name of the Lord.
Hosanna in the highest.]

With hands extended, he continues:

God our Father,   *Celebrant alone*
all over the world your people praise you.
So now we pray with the whole Church:
with N., our pope and N., our bishop.
In heaven the blessed Virgin Mary,
the apostles and all the saints
always sing your praise.
Now we join with them and with the angels
to adore you as we sing (say):

*People with celebrant
and concelebrants*

All say:

Holy, holy, holy Lord, God of power and might,
heaven and earth are full of your glory.
Hosanna in the highest.
Blessed is he who comes in the name of the Lord.
Hosanna in the highest.

With hands extended, he says:

G od our Father,
you are most holy
and we want to show you that we are grateful.

Celebrant alone

W e bring you bread and wine

Celebrant alone or
with concelebrants

He joins his hands. All concelebrants with hands outstretched over the offerings, say:

and ask you to send your Holy Spirit to make these gifts

The celebrant joins his hands and, making the sign of the cross once over both bread and chalice, says:

the body ✛ and blood of Jesus your Son.

With hands joined, they continue:

Then we can offer to you
what you have given to us.

O n the night before he died,
Jesus was having supper with his apostles.

The celebrant takes the bread and raises it a little above the altar. All continue:

He took bread from the table.
He gave you thanks and praise.
Then he broke the bread, gave it to his friends, and said:

Each extends his right hand towards the bread, if this seems opportune.

Take this, all of you, and eat it:
this is my body which will be given up for you.

At the elevation, they look at the host and afterwards bow low.

Then all continue:

When supper was ended,

The celebrant takes the chalice and raises it a little above the altar. Then all continue:

Jesus took the cup that was filled with wine.
He thanked you, gave it to his friends, and said:

Each extends his right hand towards the chalice, if this seems opportune.

Take this, all of you, and drink from it:
this is the cup of my blood,
the blood of the new and everlasting covenant.
It will be shed for you and for all
so that sins may be forgiven.
Then he said to them:
do this in memory of me.

At the elevation they look at the chalice and afterwards bow low.

Celebrant
with concelebrants

We do now what Jesus told us to do.
      We remember his death and his resurrection
and we offer you, Father, the bread that gives us life,
and the cup that saves us.
Jesus brings us to you;
welcome us as you welcome him.

Then the principal celebrant sings or says:

Let us proclaim our faith:

Celebrant alone

All say:

a. Christ has died,
Christ is risen,
Christ will come again.

People with celebrant and concelebrants

b. Dying you destroyed our death,
rising you restored our life.
Lord Jesus, come in glory.

c. When we eat this bread and drink this cup,
we proclaim your death, Lord Jesus,
until you come in glory.

d. Lord, by your cross and resurrection
you have set us free.
You are the Savior of the world.

With hands extended, all say:

Celebrant with concelebrants

**Father,
because you love us,
you invite us to come to your table.
Fill us with the joy of the Holy Spirit
as we receive the body and blood of your Son.**

With hands extended, he says:

Celebrant or one concelebrant

**Lord,
you never forget any of your children.
We ask you to take care of those we love,
especially of N. and N.,
and we pray for those who have died.**

**Remember everyone who is suffering from pain or sorrow.
Remember Christians everywhere
and all other people in the world.**

**We are filled with wonder and praise
when we see what you do for us
through Jesus your Son,
and so we sing:**

The principal celebrant takes the paten with the host and the deacon (or in his absence one of the concelebrants) takes the chalice and, lifting them up, the principal celebrant sings or says alone or with the concelebrants:

**Through him,
with him,
in him,
in the unity of the Holy Spirit,
all glory and honor is yours,
almighty Father,
for ever and ever.**

Celebrant alone or with concelebrants

The people respond:

Amen.

EUCHARISTIC PRAYER
FOR MASSES WITH CHILDREN

II

Priest: **The Lord be with you.**
People: And also with you.

Priest: **Lift up your hearts.**
People: We lift them up to the Lord.

Priest: **Let us give thanks to the Lord our God.**
People: It is right to give him thanks and praise.

The principal celebrant, with hands extended, says:

**God, our loving Father,
we are glad to give you thanks and praise
because you love us.
With Jesus we sing your praise:**

Celebrant alone

All say:

Glory to God in the highest.
> or:
Hosanna in the highest.

*People with celebrant
and concelebrants*

The principal celebrant says:

**Because you love us,
you gave us this great and beautiful world.
With Jesus we sing your praise:**

All say:

Glory to God in the highest.
> or:
Hosanna in the highest.

*People with celebrant
and concelebrants*

The celebrant says:

Because you love us,
you sent Jesus your Son
to bring us to you
and to gather us around him
as the children of one family.
With Jesus we sing your praise:

All say:

Glory to God in the highest.

> People with celebrant
> and concelebrants

or:

Hosanna in the highest.

The principal celebrant says:

For such great love
we thank you with the angels and saints
as they praise you and sing (say):

> People with celebrant
> and concelebrants

All say:

Holy, holy, holy Lord, God of power and might,
heaven and earth are full of your glory.
Hosanna in the highest.
Blessed is he who comes in the name of the Lord.
Hosanna in the highest.

With hands extended, he says:

Blessed be Jesus, whom you sent
to be the friend of children and of the poor.

> Celebrant alone

He came to show us
how we can love you, Father,
by loving one another.
He came to take away sin,
which keeps us from being friends,
and hate, which makes us all unhappy.

He promised to send the Holy Spirit,
to be with us always
so that we can live as your children.

All say:

Blessed is he who comes in the name of the Lord.
    Hosanna in the highest.

All concelebrants, with hands outstretched over the offerings, say:

**God our Father,
we now ask you
to send your Holy Spirit
to change these gifts of bread and wine
into the body ✛ and blood
of Jesus Christ, our Lord.**

They join their hands.

**The night before he died,
Jesus your Son showed us how much you love us.
When he was at supper with his disciples,
he took bread,
and gave you thanks and praise.
Then he broke the bread,
gave it to his friends, and said:**

Each extends his right hand towards the bread, if this seems opportune.

**Take this, all of you, and eat it:
This is my body which will be given up for you.**

Jesus has given his life for us.

At the elevation they look at the host and afterwards bow low.

Then all continue:

*Celebrant
with concelebrants*

When supper was ended,
    Jesus took the cup that was filled with wine.
He thanked you, gave it to his friends, and said:

Each extends his right hand towards the chalice, if this seems opportune.

**Take this, all of you, and drink from it:
this is the cup of my blood,
the blood of the new and everlasting covenant.
It will be shed for you and for all
so that sins may be forgiven.**

All say:

*People with celebrant
and concelebrants*

Jesus has given his life for us.

*Celebrant
with concelebrants*

**Then he said to them:
do this in memory of me.**

At the elevation they look at the chalice and afterwards bow low.

With hands extended, all say:

*Celebrant
with concelebrants*

And so, loving Father,
    we remember that Jesus died and rose again
to save the world.
He put himself into our hands
to be the sacrifice we offer you.

All say:

People with celebrant and concelebrants

We praise you, we bless you, we thank you.

With hands extended, all say:

Celebrant with concelebrants

**Lord our God
listen to our prayer.
Send the Holy Spirit
to all of us who share in this meal.
May this Spirit bring us closer together
in the family of the Church,
with N., our pope,
N., our bishop,
all other bishops,
and all who serve your people.**

All say:

People with celebrant and concelebrants

We praise you, we bless you, we thank you.

With hands extended, he says:

Celebrant or one concelebrant

**Remember, Father, our families and friends (. . .),
and all those we do not love as we should.
Remember those who have died (. . .).
Bring them home to you
to be with you for ever.**

All say:

People with celebrant and concelebrants

We praise you, we bless you, we thank you.

With hands extended, he says:

Celebrant or one concelebrant

**Gather us all together into your kingdom.
There we shall be happy for ever
with the Virgin Mary, Mother of God and our mother.
There all the friends
of Jesus the Lord
will sing a song of joy.**

All say:

People with celebrant
and concelebrants

We praise you, we bless you, we thank you.

The principal celebrant takes the paten with the host and the deacon (or in his absence one of the concelebrants) takes the chalice and, lifting them up, the principal celebrant sings or says alone or with the concelebrants:

Celebrant alone or
with concelebrants

Through him,
with him,
in him,
in the unity of the Holy Spirit,
all glory and honor is yours,
almighty Father,
for ever and ever.

The people respond:

Amen.

EUCHARISTIC PRAYER
FOR MASSES WITH CHILDREN

III

Priest: **The Lord be with you.**
People: And also with you.

Priest: **Lift up your hearts.**
People: We lift them up to the Lord.

Priest: **Let us give thanks to the Lord our God.**
People: It is right to give him thanks and praise.

The principal celebrant, with hands extended, says:

**We thank you,
God our Father.**

`Celebrant alone`

***You made us to live for you and for each other.
We can see and speak to one another,
and become friends,
and share our joys and sorrows.**

**And so, Father, we gladly thank you
with every one who believes in you;
with the saints and the angels,
we rejoice and praise you, saying:**

---

* During the Easter Season this section may be replaced by the following:

**You are the living God;
you have called us to share in your life,
and to be happy with you for ever.
You raised up Jesus, your Son,
the first among us to rise from the dead,
and gave him new life.
You have promised to give us new life also,
a life that will never end,
a life with no more anxiety and suffering.**

All say:

Holy, holy, holy Lord, God of power and might,
heaven and earth are full of your glory.
> Hosanna in the highest.
Blessed is he who comes in the name of the Lord.
> Hosanna in the highest.

With hands extended, he says:

Yes, Lord, you are holy;
you are kind to us and to all.
For this we thank you.
We thank you above all for your Son, Jesus Christ.

*You sent him into this world
because people had turned away from you
and no longer loved each other.
He opened our eyes and our hearts
to understand that we are brothers and sisters
and that you are Father of us all.

He now brings us together to one table
and asks us to do what he did.

---

* During the Easter Season this section may be replaced by the following:

He brought us the good news
of life to be lived with you for ever in heaven.
He showed us the way to that life,
the way of love.
He himself has gone that way before us.

All concelebrants, with hands outstretched over the offerings, say:

**Father,
we ask you to bless these gifts of bread and wine
and make them holy.**

They join their hands.

**Change them for us into the body ✠ and blood of Jesus Christ,
your Son.**

**On the night before he died for us,
he had supper for the last time with his disciples.
He took bread
and gave you thanks.
He broke the bread
and gave it to his friends, saying:**

Each extends his right hand towards the bread, if this seems opportune.

**Take this, all of you, and eat it:
this is my body which will be given up for you.**

he elevation, they look at the host and afterwards bow low.

Then all continue:

In the same way he took a cup of wine.
He gave you thanks
and handed the cup to his disciples, saying:

Each extends his right hand towards the chalice, if this seems opportune.

**Take this, all of you, and drink from it:
this is the cup of my blood,
the blood of the new and everlasting covenant.
It will be shed for you and for all
so that sins may be forgiven.
Then he said to them:
do this in memory of me.**

At the elevation they look at the chalice and afterwards bow low.

With hands extended, they say:

> Celebrant
> with concelebrants

God our Father,
we remember with joy
all that Jesus did to save us.
In this holy sacrifice,
which he gave as a gift to his Church,
we remember his death and resurrection.

With hands extended, he says:

> Celebrant or
> one concelebrant

Father in heaven,
accept us together with your beloved Son.
He willingly died for us,
but you raised him to life again.
We thank you and say:

All say:

> People with celebrant
> and concelebrants

Glory to God in the highest.
(Or some other suitable acclamation of praise.)

With hands extended, he says:

Celebrant or
one concelebrant

**Jesus now lives with you in glory,
but he is also here on earth, among us.
We thank you and say:**

All say:

People with celebrant
and concelebrants

Glory to God in the highest.
(Or some other suitable acclamation of praise.)

With hands extended, he says:

Celebrant or
one concelebrant

**One day he will come in glory
and in his kingdom
there will be no more suffering,
no more tears, no more sadness.
We thank you and say:**

All say:

People with celebrant
and concelebrants

Glory to God in the highest.
(Or some other suitable acclamation of praise.)

With hands extended, he says:

Celebrant or
one concelebrant

**Father in heaven,
you have called us
to receive the body and blood of Christ at this table
and to be filled with the joy of the Holy Spirit.
Through this sacred meal
give us strength to please you more and more.**

With hands extended, he says:

Celebrant or
one concelebrant

Lord, our God,
remember **N.**, our pope,
N., our bishop, and all other bishops.

* Help all who follow Jesus
to work for peace
and to bring happiness to others.

Bring us all at last
together with Mary, the Mother of God,
and all the saints,
to live with you
and to be one with Christ in heaven.

The principal celebrant takes the paten with the host and the deacon (or in his absence one of the concelebrants) takes the chalice and, lifting them up, the principal celebrant sings or says alone or with the concelebrants:

Celebrant alone or
with concelebrants

Through him,
with him,
in him,
in the unity of the Holy Spirit,
all glory and honor is yours,
almighty Father,
for ever and ever.

The people respond:

Amen.

---

* During the Easter season this section may be replaced by the following:

Fill all Christians with the gladness of Easter.
Help us to bring this joy
to all who are sorrowful.

EUCHARISTIC PRAYER
FOR MASSES OF RECONCILIATION

I

Priest: **The Lord be with you.**
People: And also with you.

Priest: **Lift up your hearts.**
People: We lift them up to the Lord.

Priest: **Let us give thanks to the Lord our God.**
People: It is right to give him thanks and praise.

The principal celebrant, with hands extended, says:

Celebrant alone

**Father, all-powerful and ever-living God,
we do well always and everywhere to give you thanks
and praise.
You never cease to call us
to a new and more abundant life.**

**God of love and mercy,
you are always ready to forgive;
we are sinners,
and you invite us
to trust in your mercy.**

**Time and time again
we broke your covenant,
but you did not abandon us.
Instead, through your Son, Jesus our Lord,
you bound yourself even more closely to the human family
by a bond that can never be broken.**

**Now is the time
for your people to turn back to you
and to be renewed in Christ your Son,
a time of grace and reconciliation.**

52

You invite us
to serve the family of mankind
by opening our hearts
to the fullness of your Holy Spirit.

In wonder and gratitude,
we join our voices with the choirs of heaven
to proclaim the power of your love
and to sing of our salvation in Christ:

All say:

*People with celebrant
and concelebrants*

Holy, holy, holy Lord, God of power and might,
heaven and earth are full of your glory.
    Hosanna in the highest.
Blessed is he who comes in the name of the Lord.
    Hosanna in the highest.

With hands extended, he says:

Celebrant alone

Father,
from the beginning of time
you have always done what is good for man
so that we may be holy as you are holy.

All concelebrants, with hands outstretched over the offerings, say:

*Celebrant
with concelebrants*

Look with kindness on your people
gathered here before you:
send forth the power of your Spirit
so that these gifts may become for us
the body ✠ and blood of your beloved Son, Jesus the Christ,
in whom we have become your sons and daughters.

They join their hands.

When we were lost
and could not find the way to you,
you loved us more than ever:
Jesus, your Son, innocent and without sin,
gave himself into our hands
and was nailed to a cross.
Yet before he stretched out his arms between heaven and
    earth
in the everlasting sign of your covenant,
he desired to celebrate the Paschal feast
in the company of his disciples.

While they were at supper,
he took bread and gave you thanks and praise.
He broke the bread, gave it to his disciples, and said:

Each extends his right hand towards the bread, if this seems opportune.

**Take this, all of you, and eat it:
this is my body which will be given up for you.**

At the elevation they look at the host and afterwards bow low.

Then all continue:

At the end of the meal,
knowing that he was to reconcile all things in himself
by the blood of his cross,
he took the cup, filled with wine.
Again he gave you thanks, handed the cup to his friends,
    and said:

Each extends his right hand towards the chalice, if this seems opportune.

Take this, all of you, and drink from it:
this is the cup of my blood,
the blood of the new and everlasting covenant.
It will be shed for you and for all
so that sins may be forgiven.
Do this in memory of me.

At the elevation they look at the chalice and afterwards bow low.

> Celebrant alone

Let us proclaim the mystery of faith:

a. Christ has died,
Christ is risen,
Christ will come again.

> People with celebrant and concelebrants

b. Dying you destroyed our death,
rising you restored our life.
Lord Jesus, come in glory.

c. When we eat this bread and drink this cup,
we proclaim your death, Lord Jesus,
until you come in glory.

d. Lord, by your cross and resurrection
you have set us free.
You are the Savior of the world.

With hands extended, all say:

> Celebrant
> with concelebrants

**We do this in memory of Jesus Christ,
our Passover and our lasting peace.
We celebrate his death and resurrection
and look for the coming of that day
when he will return to give us the fullness of joy.
Therefore we offer you, God ever faithful and true,
the sacrifice which restores man to your friendship.**

**Father,
look with love
on those you have called
to share in the one sacrifice of Christ.
By the power of your Holy Spirit
make them one body,
healed of all division.**

With hands extended, he says:

> Celebrant or
> one concelebrant

**Keep us all
in communion of mind and heart
with N., our pope, and N., our bishop.*
Help us to work together
for the coming of your kingdom,
until at last we stand in your presence
to share the life of the saints,
in the company of the Virgin Mary and the apostles
and of our departed brothers and sisters
whom we commend to your mercy.**

**Then, freed from every shadow of death,
we shall take our place in the new creation
and give you thanks
with Christ, our risen Lord.**

---

* When several are to be named, a general form is used: for N. our bishop
and his assistant bishops, as in number 172 of the General Instruction.

The principal celebrant takes the paten with the host and the deacon (or in his absence one of the concelebrants) takes the chalice and, lifting them up, the principal celebrant sings or says alone or with the concelebrants:

Through him,
  with him,
in him,
in the unity of the Holy Spirit,
all glory and honor is yours,
almighty Father,
for ever and ever.

*Celebrant alone or
with concelebrants*

The people respond:

Amen.

EUCHARISTIC PRAYER
FOR MASSES OF RECONCILIATION

II

Priest: **The Lord be with you.**
People: And also with you.

Priest: **Lift up your hearts.**
People: We lift them up to the Lord.

Priest: **Let us give thanks to the Lord our God.**
People: It is right to give him thanks and praise.

The principal celebrant, with hands extended, says:

Celebrant alone

**Father, all-powerful and ever-living God,
we praise and thank you through Jesus Christ our Lord
for your presence and action in the world.**

**In the midst of conflict and division,
we know it is you
who turn our minds to thoughts of peace.
Your Spirit changes our hearts:
enemies begin to speak to one another,
those who were estranged join hands in friendship,
and nations seek the way of peace together.**

**Your Spirit is at work
when understanding puts an end to strife,
when hatred is quenched by mercy,
and vengeance gives way to forgiveness.**

**For this we should never cease
to thank and praise you.
We join with all the choirs of heaven
as they sing for ever to your glory:**

All say:

People with celebrant
and concelebrants

Holy, holy, holy Lord, God of power and might.
Heaven and earth are full of your glory.
    Hosanna in the highest.
Blessed is he who comes in the name of the Lord.
    Hosanna in the highest.

With hands extended, he says:

Celebrant alone

God of power and might,
we praise you through your Son, Jesus Christ,
who comes in your name.
He is the Word that brings salvation.
He is the hand you stretch out to sinners.
He is the way that leads to your peace.

God our Father,
we had wandered far from you,
but through your Son you have brought us back.
You gave him up to death
so that we might turn again to you
and find our way to one another.

All concelebrants, with hands outstretched over the offerings, say:

Celebrant
with concelebrants

Therefore we celebrate the reconciliation
Christ has gained for us.

We ask you to sanctify these gifts
by the power of your Spirit,
as we now fulfill your Son's ✠ command.

They join their hands.

**While he was at supper
on the night before he died for us,**

Each extends his right hand towards the bread, if this seems opportune.

**he took bread in his hands,
and gave you thanks and praise.
He broke the bread,
gave it to his disciples, and said:**

**Take this, all of you, and eat it:
this is my body which will be given up for you.**

At the elevation, they look at the host and afterwards bow low.

Then all continue:

**At the end of the meal he took the cup.
Again he praised you for your goodness,
gave the cup to his disciples, and said:**

Each extends his right hand towards the chalice, if this seems opportune.

**Take this, all of you, and drink from it:
this is the cup of my blood,
the blood of the new and everlasting covenant.
It will be shed for you and for all
so that sins may be forgiven.
Do this in memory of me.**

At the elevation they look at the chalice and afterwards bow low.

Let us proclaim the mystery of faith:

Celebrant alone

*People with celebrant
and concelebrants*

a.   Christ has died,
     Christ is risen,
     Christ will come again.

b.   Dying you destroyed our death,
     rising you restored our life.
     Lord Jesus, come in glory.

c.   When we eat this bread and drink this cup,
     we proclaim your death, Lord Jesus,
     until you come in glory.

d.   Lord, by your cross and resurrection
     you have set us free.
     You are the Savior of the world.

With hands extended, all say:

*Celebrant
with concelebrants*

Lord our God,
your Son has entrusted to us
this pledge of his love.
We celebrate the memory of his death and resurrection
and bring you the gift you have given us,
the sacrifice of reconciliation.
Therefore, we ask you, Father,
to accept us, together with your Son.

Fill us with his Spirit
through our sharing in this meal.
May he take away all that divides us.

With hands extended, he says:

Celebrant or
one concelebrant

**May this Spirit keep us always in communion
with N., our pope, N., our bishop,***
with all the bishops and all your people.
Father, make your Church throughout the world
a sign of unity and an instrument of your peace.

You have gathered us here
around the table of your Son,
in fellowship with the Virgin Mary, Mother of God, and all
the saints.

In that new world where the fullness of your peace will be
revealed,
gather people of every race, language, and way of life
to share in the one eternal banquet
with Jesus Christ the Lord.

The principal celebrant takes the paten with the host and the deacon (or in his absence one of the concelebrants) takes the chalice and, lifting them up, the principal celebrant sings or says alone or with the concelebrants:

Celebrant alone or
with concelebrants

Through him,
with him,
in him,
in the unity of the Holy Spirit,
all glory and honor is yours,
almighty Father,
for ever and ever.

The people respond:

Amen.

---

* When several are to he named, a general form is used: for N. our bishop and his assistant bishops, as in number 172 of the General Instruction.

THE APOSTLES' CREED

In celebrations of Masses with children, the Apostles' Creed may be said after the homily.

I believe in God, the Father almighty,
creator of heaven and earth.

I believe in Jesus Christ, his only Son, our Lord.
He was conceived by the power of the Holy Spirit
and born of the Virgin Mary.
He suffered under Pontius Pilate,
was crucified, died, and was buried.
He descended to the dead.
On the third day he rose again.
He ascended into heaven,
and is seated at the right hand of the Father.
He will come again to judge the living and the dead.

I believe in the Holy Spirit,
the holy catholic Church,
the communion of saints,
the forgiveness of sins,
the resurrection of the body,
and the life everlasting. Amen.